In the Mercy of Snow

In the Mercy of Snow

Poems by

Elizabeth Balise

Cover design by Shay Culligan

ISBN: 978-1-63980-023-0

Kelsay Books
502 South 1040 East, A-119
American Fork, Utah 84003
Kelsaybooks.com

Dedicated to my daughters, Phoebe and Andrea—

with all my love

Acknowledgments

With gratitude to these first publishers of my works:

Ariel Chart: "Middle Archaic Spear Point"
The Blue Nib: "Moon Metal," "I Will Deal with This Tomorrow"
  "The Mayor of Wesson Street"
Mothers Always Write: "Yellow Waking Mother"
Thirteen Myna Birds: "Raking Under Forsythia"

Many thanks go to my friend and mentor, Barbara Hoffman, and fellow poet Mike Griffith for their help and steadfast encouragement in producing this book. Thanks also go to Jim Cunningham, an accomplished storyteller, and poet who took the time to write a review.

Contents

I First Saw Scranton   11
Middle Archaic Spear Point   13
Moon Metal   15
Jazz Virgin   16
Milky Way Moment   18
Nap   19
For Henrietta Swan—   20
Henrietta Swan Leavitt   22
Bicycle Daydream   23
The Mayor of Wesson Street   25
Burgundy   28
Sunset Apology   30
Luis   31
Samaras of a Silver Maple   34
Target Ship 1966   35
Yellow Waking Mother   37
It's There   40
Flood Stage   41
Somewhere Else   43
Raking Under Forsythia   46
Where I Left Them   47
I Will Deal with This Tomorrow   50
Purple   52
Downsizing   54
Sigh Differently   57
Pulling Off My Scarf   58
Hunting Poems   59
Stand-Off   60
Ercel's House 1969   63
Against Itself   64
Night Skating at Porter Lake   66
The Request   69
Only Snow Will Do   71
Signed Her Name   73

I First Saw Scranton

…and did not unpack
my life

as if it were always meant to be a ruin

I first saw Scranton
Not much of a view
beyond the smoldering mountains of culm
dumps decrepit
Mills tethered to the whistle
of the Lace Works and
once prosperous coal
City in denial

Decay of Great mansions—abandoned
on the Hill

Away

from spit and clap-board
hovels of miners
in the barren
mud beside the river
below
And I remember thinking

"How can I ever live here?"

I own one of those houses now
fifty years—under foot and harnessed
in the stays of whale bone and lace

of that certain stench of starch
on muggy days

Just another in a string of small sad
cities'
people
so used
and waiting
to be
covered
once again
by heaviness

Its sin
in the mercy of snow…

Middle Archaic Spear Point

—For Rick

As for what you look like
now that distance and the years
can calculate the damage…

I fell in love with the man who wrote the poetry
I see him by the ocean in the moonlight
and at his family's graves
I see him in the high pasture of his home
Wading in the creek
Fragrance of his mother's roses
drifting…
in his father's laughter

As his brother sleeps-in
—forever

I see you drinking coffee
little Bobo, on your lap
Stars reflect
chihuahua-huge
devotion
in his limpid, darling eyes

I see you, sullen one
whom I would have followed
just to know you...
curious
in some foreign forest
so far south of my accent
lost in time and purpose there in Georgia—

…and what were you thinking
while waiting for your son?

And what else?
Only God could know the rest…

I see you in the moon that pulls the tides
across the ages
till our eyes meet in your words—a piercing

so unexpected

Moon Metal

She rises above the bay
on her wake—a Tenebrae of carbon
Then bolts back
careening 'cross blue-black—
through her lucent clouds of hair
from which on radii spray a diaspora of stars
Mistress of Metallurgy
tempered, tampering
Darkness forged to alloy with light

Men have always wondered
how anything could be so round...

To arouse a sullen tide
her fingers palpate night-water's lead
tingling light of limbs so spread
to her lover!

Close him in—
a pewter path of trembling touches
that ends in the small of her back

Men so wooed, still shudder
"How anything so tender...?"

...could expose such stone!

She eclipses the sun!
She commands the sky!
...to hone his steel on that!

Jazz Virgin

Susan
with her china-white skin
relaxed
down to lace bra and panties—

"Have you ever heard this?" she asks

...sets the album, drops the needle
in the groove
We wait till bass fills in the room
sending time and silence empty-handed
down a hallway

Susan lights a joint
settles on the bed
ample legs begging apart
She sucks in deeply
impounding clouds
Head thrown back
Thick glossy hair—
loses gravity
Eyes half-closed, shadow-heavy
clear and blue like piano
The walls are muted trumpet
stutter-hush of cymbal and the snare

Crackling over scratches

We are barely there

Susan exhales
a swirl of fog below a frail moon
Only her sultry voice still holds me tethered

16

"Have you ever heard anything—like this?"

Miles flows
around me
Smoking
On the floor of Susan's room
lying clothed and drunk
Soaked
with chords and wonder

I never hear him coming

Miles takes his time....

Milky Way Moment

Seldom seen in the stew of Scranton skies

But there it is—
a rubber band of fog

smudged across black distance…
Myriad-multitudes
They are truly there!

Each burning ball
 gathered beyond my imagination

by the Moon Mother

Who scrubs the faces
of her little stars

Nap

A blue jay
cries in deep background
of robin's qweedle day

A breeze moves the curtains slightly

Sun-light scrawls
its shadows soothing brighter
Lolling on a cushion
of late afternoon

and mourning dove
calls
to its mate

Meet her
on the edge
of sleep

For Henrietta Swan—

Henrietta
dark-eyed darling of the night sky—

A Swan
who sails
the heavens
deaf with lights
that pulse across your mind
In photographic plates
that number
many thousands

You see the differential of light
You swim the curves that grace the arch of heaven
between the cloud and pinwheel galaxies

You measure
their exquisite wakes of distance—
Become the glittering timepiece of the farthest stars—

Bestowed forever in your hands

the clock and keys of all existence

You know the bend of ages

You heard the voices of the light

of angels
and of man

I hope you've found true happiness
gathered to your love
forgetful of the pond of space and time
and all that hopeless pain and counting
of perfection

and of loneliness

to which you were assigned

that in your hands unravel all....
The secrets of the universe
white and silver whorls in motion...
brilliant beyond all measure
by which you were forgotten
and unvalued by design

Eulogized only—
as loving God
and as being kind

Henrietta Swan Leavitt

The concept for the measurement of light years was first accurately calculated from the study of thousands of photographic plates of cepheid stars and their variable brightness by Henrietta Swan Leavitt—a bean counter (human computer) in the employ of The Harvard Observatory under the direction of Charles Pickering at the beginning of the 20th century. Later, her research was picked up by Edwin Hubble to determine that the universe was not static but actually expanding.

She was a well-educated woman, who in spite of being mostly deaf from childhood illnesses, would have earned the Nobel Prize in the field of astronomy for her determined efforts—if it were not for her untimely death. She was nominated, but the award is not given posthumously.

Her colleague, Solon I. Bailey wrote in her obituary: "She had the happy faculty of appreciating all that was worthy and lovable in others and was possessed of a nature so full of sunshine that, to her, all of life became beautiful and full of meaning."

Bicycle Daydream

Somewhere between a bicycle
and a seat at a daydream…

I had to make money
so I mortgaged
my woods, my sea, my music
my words—

and left…

Regaled only with rust and memory

My 1938 Columbia bike
sold for a crib
to an antiques dealer
Fat-tires, red-faded fenders
Baskets saddled over wheel

for towel, lunchbox

Key chain jangling
against jar
of cool ginger ale

Looking back at them now—
filled with afternoons at the park

I was almost a poet

The road laid itself bare
before my bike and me
scrolling through leaves

like words that fell
like hair blown across shoulders
that I sang to no one—to everyone

The audience then—
was air

I know that now

I was not really…nor ready

…I was always a poet

The Mayor of Wesson Street

Not the lone glory of an orange
basking in Depression's dusk—
its fluted bowl of purple glass

Not the fall ways of amber
Leaves burned by roadside
curling smoke's sun-lit sash

Not tree-lined streets
rabid leaves' raspy voices
whirling giddy in the wind—

...in none of these

But in the moments I filled with fixing
a lamp shade
painting this place
to a stern perfection
I thought of you

ordering the tyranny of me
the glass of me
the concrete conscience
I must be right! Mustn't I?

The religion of our lives
Driving through Sundays with Polkas blaring
feeding the ducks
and a roast at noon
Waffles and TV later
Lassie and *You Asked for It!*
Wiping my mouth on a Sunday sleeve

I asked for it, alright

He came and went
to the smell of Ice Blue Aqua Velva

He came and went larger than life and first on the scene
to hurricanes, fires, muggings, and races
and of course—THE SHOP!
in an amazing array of uniforms and vehicles
Ambulances, wreckers, pickups, and police cars

He was terrifying! Wonderful!

We would love at a pained distance

His cabinet in the cellar was always locked

But now, just suppose—
if a kid were to haul on its handles…
supposedly—the sheet metal would heave and roar
with the thunder of him!

And those late nights
those harsh bookie lights
lidded hundred-watt cones
in the spotlight of THERE
where I wasn't
in the odor of oils too noxious to dare
beyond the girlish shadows—

he cleaned his guns

I waited and watched where everything seemed
to be what…?
it seems—he just pushed her against a wall!

I step from girlhood
with my two-cents worth
and it seems I will not be *Queen for a Day!*

I take my vows!
I swear I will not scrape wax
from the corner of the kitchen floor with a knife!

I have waited. I have watched
the routines of his mornings
He's brushing his teeth; he's combing his hair
He's tying his shoes while he chats with the cat
I can tell you the creak of the stairs
and the sound of his footsteps rounding the house

…the routine of his return at supper
the routine of anger
My routine of being late—
and as good as dead
squeezing behind—
HIS CHAIR
Praying he wouldn't notice the mud
Praying for the epiphany of his good mood
when the TV and me

wouldn't be blamed for the downfall of the nation

Burgundy

Burgundy, the color of a dress I've never worn
to an occasion that never occurred

Velvet lined
coffin
Where lies the violin
There lies its song

The heart of fiddle strings
that bare of arms
That heart that sings, speaks, no, yells
to the hands that can't respond!
to a mind that can't remember
I was drowning in some future
not a violinist's

"Alive with Pleasure"
read the billboard slogan for cigarettes
behind the happy couple
running out into their future

Forcing the hand of marriage
Waving goodbye to my life
from a rooftop in Scranton
as the wind hauled my laundry three city blocks
dumping my unders on Saint Luke's sills
sailing my sheets up Wyoming Ave.

I lay on the tar and pebble roof
watching pigeons swirl
listening to traffic pass on the street below
The moment you know you've made the mistake
you can't return from…

Wherever my towels have blown?
I wish them well…

Sunset Apology

I hold your life inside my womb
as you hold me
in your sea of seeds and wavery reeds
Beach grass on breast of sand

Ripples of wind
Across my dune

drifts...
your hand

Tracing the mark of a high tide
with my wanderings
Will I be the last?
to recall its highest reach upon the land?

I note the smell of dead and ebb
Would change it all on my return
if it were up to me

And once I started running out
"Wait! O Wait!"

Black breaks
The sand bars
between the tide pool's
red whispers of you

I now believe
gulls turn time in their wings

Luis

Luis was lured from a chicken coup
by a cold lunch-meat sandwich
Luis who knew nothing of clothes or care
nor when to eat
nor what to wear
Nor who to love

or how to plead

nor what to say
nor how to say it

Where does love go...?

Sweet love...

...for the boy
become man,
"mentally challenged"
of a Mom, "mentally challenged"
confined to the scraps...
in that hospital
of days...of years
such as they were...

of cold and lack
of anything approaching care

At a group home at last
with what was allotted, allowed
In a room shared by only one other
A record by Patsy
played over and over and over again—

"…Crazy, I'm crazy for feeling so lonely
I'm crazy, crazy—for feeling so blue…" *

(keep hearing the rhythms and tune of this song)

Why might—your little heart be so broken?
Till the Sunlight came in
in the face of a woman
The "Mommy"
of dinners
and Christmas
and music
and showers and bedtime

of dropping your pants in the bank for attention of
"Mommy!"

whose scoldings you craved
whose lap was your pillow
for flicking your earlobe
to smiles and the giggles and singing
so desperately missed
as she washed the dishes—

"The Mommy"

of part time and sometime
of someone
who loved you a while
while she could
in the aching of life

For what it meant for a moment
to Luis—
a lifetime of love in your voice
that the angels of heaven could never replace

so they envy

So you go

so she comes
to you Luis

a gift
of the God
who could never forget you

"…I'm crazy for trying and crazy for crying
And I'm crazy for loving you"

To my daughter Phoebe, "the bright and shiny one,"
—for the time she gave in this group home.
She worked there and loved them:
Luis, Alan, and John. I am unspeakably proud.

…And, to all the under-appreciated
and caring residence workers everywhere.

Samaras of a Silver Maple

A winged seed just took to wind
and landed on my lap
like hope and babies—
I imagine
I've not had

In memories
of walking home from school in May

Stunned by design
Perfect curl of comma
veined and paper
-thin
skin with spine
of strength attached
to guide its flight
of swirling fertile
to the grounded mind

To love—
the tan and winged snow
in dizzy dance
from height of trees

on both sides of this moment

a child
in a future forest

Target Ship 1966

Black, Swiss-cheese hulk on horizon
The James Longstreet
immobile old freighter of the bay
towed to the ignominy
of its last commission
in the curled arm of Cape Cod
Tides flex their muscles against it
But The Longstreet is steadfast
in its dark purpose

Standing target for practice

A sortie if planes home in on its bulk
Honing their skills
on this fish-in-a-barrel
Thunderheads etched—inflammatory
booming follows the miles over water

Against The Longstreet's silhouette enduring
even God takes aim
firing bolts across its bow
Taking aim at our futures

Standing targets for practice

Vietnam? Cape Cod?

No difference to teens
before life's ocean of conscription

Sand is cold beneath dunes
Beach grass rustles
to the pulsing surf
to the wind's rhythms

just below hearing
as if there's a secret
that must be kept

We are targets for practice
We are meaningless din

Pulling our sweatshirts and blanket closer
The Supremes sing thinly
from transistor

"Stopped, for a moment—
in the name of love"

Thinking it over

Yellow Waking Mother

Yellow is
a high-minded mood
extravagant sunlight
to be touched—
not long
by the colors of play

for a child of seven

It is hair tendering golden-
brown pennies for lemonade

Yellow is
bumping into the screaming end
of a lit cigarette

Yellow is
dripping from the eaves
onto an empty soup can

It is
spindling sparrow song
from highest perch on roof
his pitch can attain

Yellow is
in rattled doorknob
An infant's sweet
voice wanting—in
Reciting menu
above mattress
edges into sleep

Two dark eyes plead for yellow—
waking Mother into morning's—
"juice…eggs"

Yellow is
a car door opening
on the shore's unmistakable!
Smells of life
warmth and breeze
Touching strings
the kites
of sense
harmonics above the tone
Octaves of excitement
to see to hear to touch to taste

to know
again—the ocean of my mother
as she calms the restless waves and sand of us
with stuff to lug out to the beach
towels, pails and shovels
Picnic basket, cooler
lotion, comic books, her magazines

Mom looks out
Her glasses, dark
Preside
reflecting beauty—

"Take your sister's hand."

Yellow is the squeal
of cannot wait

This poem appeared in the online journal
Mothers Always Write, October 2019.

It's There

It's there—
in our goodbye
in that last glance back
across the heat reflecting
from the roof
Your car between us
The door is open—
and your wounded soul

He's dead at 21—I know
you loved him

I overdose this moment

Paralyzed

our eyes—

go on forever

Flood Stage

Later at the same address
A storm of words reaches flood stage
A couch is bobbing in the currents
towards its mangled ruin-nexus
matchsticks in cyclonic flow
amidst the renegade trash
dangling from the limbs
of trees so festooned along the bank

Meanwhile—
chair heaved through her door

Like the river
I am not above my rage
at this stage
of more-than-enough…

Clever daughter's got my goat

Turns my words on dimes

Lays into me
her score of blame
Each blow to drop me further

presses all my buttons at one time
despite the flashing
Warning! Warning!

"Fine! Fine!"

She blows out through the afternoon
right past me
in a torrent of curses
A stubborn perfect storm
of words
has taken out parental dam
and blown out toward the Bay of Freedom
to the sorrows of her day

The river may crack its whip
But its got nothing on her

Nothing is left standing
in her way

Somewhere Else

Remembering My first taste of coffee—
just another commodity
standing outside Lowell Tech or local factory
a city corner in Haverhill snows—a worker's town
Passing out leaflets for a vapid Revolution
Another action/demonstration
to "Seize the Day!"

No computers; no social media
to fill the ranks of rallies at that time
So we froze our asses off
trying to explain with frosted breath
and fogs of rhetoric

A truth—so tyrannic, remote, arcane
too preposterous to even process
let alone explain

Standing there behind
its barbed wire reality
smoking from its stacks
the poisons of its process
and our day

Standing there
Stamping blood into my feet
Trying to convince my freezing self
my breaking heart
that all this truth?
was truly worth it?
as I threw my education and my life away—
Trying to convince those workers

...that inside that building
IT—was being made

Napalm and
that Agent of Death and Defoliation
of an orange
persuasion so our war could have its way
with rice paddies, jungles
and people—browner, poorer, smaller

While on the home-front
we filled the mills with unwilling bodies
that died later
somewhere else
offsite...

...or maybe some years down the line
from toxins dumped in rivers
left to leach to cancers
somewhere else

Into the ground they sink
Through tentacled subsidiaries
downsized by robots
and restructured divestments
Statutes of limitations
Legal dismissals
of responsibility
as the players run
for loopholes in the law

One fast move after another
they dissolve disperse
morph into another

renamed shitty entity
Clean up their storefronts
clean out our pockets
while "providing jobs"
"investing in community"
along the way
Putting on a Goodwill Tour

sponsoring the locals
Then
taking it away

"What? We never said…"

We'll take you down!
leaving only the stench behind

Raking Under Forsythia

Who knows what stops the heart of a song
I take note

of tiny thud—
robin in the wheel well of my car

the limp head
of a cat's prey

sigh of wings
defrocked by power lines

baby starling's fledgling flight
falling short of a pond's edge

That slate morsel unearthed
by the tines of my rake

…and the world is vacant for a moment…

Grief sucks a womb of air
but how it lives—I cannot say
Upended creature of us

Stops the throbs that herald life

This poem appeared in the online journal
13 Myna Birds, October 2020.

Where I Left Them

I know where I put them

that small pile of lovely
underthings
in the back of a drawer
Stuffed away
from my every day
not fit nor fitting
anymore
for an evening
or…

Can't bring myself
to throw them out
Hope is something
you just don't…

'cause ya never know
when life might pick you up
spin ya round
where it left off
so long ago—

or something like…
that

But anyway—
I came across them
…on that first

truly warm day of spring
splayed across the mountains
of New York on my way back to PA

Driving through those
Scalloped edges not quite yellow
shy of green
Lace in layers
close to shedding heaven

or from storm's
oblique winds shredding that sheen on the foothills
from the humid cool
of earlier that day

Spring knows
right
where she put them

Spring knows exactly what to do
with golden light
…and songs'…

preposterous possibilities
of bloom

Frothy silver
creeps amid the white
reflecting light

in every threaded islet
between the mountains' stream
flows sheer silk voile
overlain with mauve and pink

Those French knots and ribbons
thrill the edges of the road
reaching through the heated veil
of longing for the gauzy air

Dogwood hands
to sooth the swelling
clouds
above—so pleading—

Please…

to touch that dark
of naked woods
below

…where I left them

…apparently

I Will Deal with This Tomorrow

I hear it
half in the bag of blankets
with an empty glass of wine
dumped
Between my thighs—
the furnace rumbling on
cat purring on my lap

"What the hell!"

That foreign sound!
…of water in the winter?
Far too cold for rain
more like a forest stream's refrain
I start to think of birds—Then it occurs—

I have a problem in the basement!

Wading into the waters of Lake Laundry
Glancing warily for those wires overhead
suspended from their rafter limbs
about to spit and snag me
with their lightning strike

Slamming that button
to make it go—
away—

Defeat dripping off
jeans and unders
A clothesline pinned with curses

Ah yes.
The smell of the Tide…
going out on another day

Purple

I cannot pick a color
I love more
Each is thrilling
and some seem
the breath of life to all the rest
I loved my crayons
They became my escape
from misery
the contrast to any given day at school

Any excuse to use them all
or just one
to avoid that lowest reading group
the monstrosities of math
If I couldn't sing it

there would be no letters in the alphabet
I could not tell you A from Z

But you see—
That day was
Purple!

That was all that mattered
I loved its richness and its depth

its mystery
its royalty
King Midas would've liked it, I was sure
Almost a religion
Vestments of the priest
in the times of expectation

It is the explanation for the last of day

As a five-year-old
I drew my love for purple
Passionate
and outside all the lines—off onto the desk
I was so proud!

But—Miss Platt, so horrified asked

"What is it…?"
I was trying to do?

I didn't know.…

I was suddenly ashamed
and frightened too

Downsizing

She hushes me repeatedly
as if my voice could be—too loud
for these shrunken, elder walls
What voice can I revive to tell her
that this little place…reminds me…?

       Ratchet up
       the young mistakes
       my welfare "townhouse"

as if my voice could be too loud!

Where does anger go to say
"These cheesy rugs remind me!"
of the smoky halls, stoop-sittin'
head lice, cock roach—
fumigated invasion
Music loud enough to blow pipes
induce trauma through the walls
Thud Crash
"Stupid fuck!"
Knife-weildin', drug-dealin', boyfriend-of-a-future

       A can of beer later…
       with stress on hold
       the smells of dinner—all fifteen of them, now!
       assault me through the front window

"Ya there yet?"
…to this "cute little apartment," I mean?

So it's sold…
Someone else will wash windows, rake the yard
Shovel Massachusetts snow

> Christmas lights come down
> in my mind—
> Running toward them still
> Toes numb
> Skates bouncing on my back
> Sled firing off sparks against the sidewalk in my wake
> Running and as always late
> Mittens soaked, heavy
> Like my eyes—

Mom and I
looking out this window for the last time
Looking out toward the daughter of the woods I was
Behind—me
the bride sinks
to the bare mattress—
"Was it really 57 years?
How can it be?"

> …since…clutching can opener and Coke
> He scooped her up and through that door.…

"How can it be? Oh my…"

"You can always keep the memories."
she chirps, to check the tears

But I can't taste them!
> …Mom baking cookies
> stew and dumplings on the stove

Snitching chocolate bits
waiting for the bowl
Impatient little helpers at her side

Colors slipping…
    A child husks corn in sunlight
    A blue Huffy gleams behind birthday candles
    Sheets billow from the line

Sounds fading…
    A choir of music boxes
    before the Christmas carnage
    Doing dishes in three-part harmony

I can barely wrap my words around our voices!

"You can always keep the memories"

Preamble to the dutiful decision
Hypothermic excuse
to dump the place

Street sign shrinking in the rearview

Sigh Differently

Tired clump of night
in the moon's slight of hand
in the moon's slight—
place to hang my hat.…

Winter clouds come tumbling toward
the gray
Raked clean by barren trees
Yard waits with its leaves
tucked in corners by the wind
along hedges, stairways
mingling with renegade trash
Stuffed in layers like elderly keepsakes for—

My yard—a neglect of winter woods
but for towels waving stiffly on the line
and the squealing crackle of my footsteps—
Being there

Stairs sigh differently coming home

Blind search for a key hole
I could die searching!
the frustrations of the blind
the fumblings of "locked out!"
I—know where to go.…

Pretend
in my warm lonely
fling mittens on the table
Survey the dirty dishes…and
close my eyes

Pulling Off My Scarf

Pulling off my scarf
letting it drape like a resignation
across the back of a chair
The sun is setting
the room is dim
and almost orange—
and is sometimes lonely
in its loss of day

I think of you now—

and then

We are walking with our arms around each other
Always...

through the Boston Commons
The air drizzled
with late-winter melt

the cobbles wet

The sounds of our steps
go on—
forever....

I turn to hang my coat

Night replaces you again

Hunting Poems

They are wild things
Sometimes, I swear
I need a shotgun
but, so as not—
to hurt the words

I hack them out of weeds
Break the ice to drag them out
Throw rocks at them in trees

Turn around three times fast
and collapse
Sometimes I catch one
still spinning dizzy
floating circle-words in breeze

I command nothing

The poems always have their way

I command nothing!

Not love—Not time—
Nor hate
Nor sun—
but the moonrise—
maybe

…in dream-light

Stand-Off

Katydids and fireflies have the levee tonight
Swat team held the day

There is peace now—
as peeping neighbors
emptying horror
among themselves
in whispers
left to wonder
'bout the chaos and the barking
of earlier that day

"Put down your weapon and come out
with your hands up!"

Again and again
the demand
"Surrender…!"

Total

There is no other way

"Let them go!
Come out! Come out with your hands up!
It'll be okay"

…and he argues in his mind with the shame and loss
…and the shame and…

"No…It will not be okay!"

He had hit her!
Hit her with his Gun

again and again…with the Gun
of his demands
The Gun of his power
to make her!
The Gun of his despair

He had hit her

The dogs are barking;
His children scream!

"Put down the gun and come out
with your hands up!"
How many more times will they say it!
for all the neighbors to hear
on a loud speaker

"Surrender!"
In front of his children?

Had she cheated?
Had he lost his job?

Could he lose any more to the screaming?
to the "junk?"

to the flashing lights?
to the window's smashing?
Fence run down?
Canisters of tear gas lobbed

into that room's stinging eyes
where there is no room
where there is no time

"I would never hurt them!
Ya know!"

"Let them go!"

"Put down your weapon and come out
with your hands up!"

It is all too loud!
It is all too much!

as he presses the gun against his temple…
explodes his loss
into the time of day

3:58 PM

Ercel's House 1969

I had been sitting on his lap
drinking beer and saying
I liked Black people—
had argued I was not a racist
It was okay for me to love or have a darker friend

Ercel touched my face with pity
allowed his thumb to graze my breast
His soft rejection in it

"You will always be a racist
You cannot love or live your way around it
Raised that way
You cannot live beyond the boundaries
of the whiteness
life has dealt you…"

"I truly hate white people," he said
"You may already know
but among them are my closest friends"

O Ercel, dear one
I want to make excuses
Searched your eyes in silence
for the answers
to your truth
found only haunting sorrow
Fifty years—
Still no reply.…

There is nothing that can undo America's history of slavery and
racial injustice except perhaps to teach the truth about it—and the
slow insistence on our humanity. Not in my lifetime.

Against Itself

Was I ten?
I think?
Was it January?
that I became distracted
by the snow's
falling silence?

The Dingle's hills lure me
off
the curving walkway toward home—

I surely know my way—
though path invisible now
but for the patterns of the trees—
I know and love…
along the skyline
Will not be lost again

My feet above its depths
Impossible
the snow
could be this deep
could take this much
should trudge so far
beyond
my breath
a fog—of all I know

I am wading in the white
warmth
in spite
of freezing
tears and reddened cheeks
Toes long since numb

...and I am, as always, late
Wipe nose on sleeve
Pull mittens with my teeth
fumbling
tissues, damp in pocket

I have gone so far...
too far
down into the Dingle's windings
and night is falling fast
Night is watching
from the hemlocks
now behind
My purpose only in
the gray of sky
the ghostly silence

I don't know where night came from
How I got there
or why I came
Only that I want to linger—
longer
than that twinge of fear

Listen to...
soft tick of snow
against itself

Wind in white pines
saddest of living things

Night Skating at Porter Lake

Lacing my skates
after walking two miles
Mom's stories of Sonia Henie

Lacing my skates
with snow-white pompoms
felt skirt
and nylon tights
Cute little hat with matching scarf
My thighs and fingers
already freezing
icy burning
from miles on foot
to get there
To the lake where—

I must get out
I must get OUT!

Knowing
What to expect from my body
the quick-twitch of muscle
could always sense
specific—
gravity of water
at 22 degrees
Desiring to feel
the motion between steel and ice
Read speed's vibrations through my body
The brain registers relation
to weather's effect

Tell of velocity
possibility of fall
Feel the slash of the blades beneath me

Throw my weight sideways sudden
to hear that furious hiss
An object in motion tending dire
to stay in motion
Threatening to stay there
always
in its heights—of speed
away—

from the crowds of skaters
swirling distant in the lights
Seeking instead
the farthest reaches of Porter Lake
speed and speed and more
to overcome
inertia
of what it is to become
undone

at the outer edges, of humanity
A force unto myself
centrifugal

Avoiding
Pregnant, slow
with years and babes

The best
must be broken
of what it takes to stay free

catching the edges with every stride
catching my toe in the quick
180 spray of frost
to the sudden still

Listen to the frigid chill
and the heave of my breath
tumbling into evidence
Gliding—
once

forever

on, into darkness
of woods on frozen water

The wildness of it all…
So infatuated with flight
so full of grace
I forgot Sonia

The moon rose
from her seat in the treetops

and applauded

The Request

Drinking wine by candle light
Small flame that might've
toasted music
Holding off instead
a flood of grief
Some wall I must retain
Some hope I still maintain
called life
...or was it love or...

one of those foolish things...

It's not important now
I am not known for caving in

Not one for asking
nor for needing much
to hold my own...

Boundless days of youth
forever slipping

Only one dream yet remains

Wash over
tender tide
The sea has found the breast
Seals it with its mouth
a hunger
plunging toward its home
of earth-warm woman

a deep surround

Longing there to cry
to take her back
to take it out on all the taking

hurt of it

The bitter
and the knowing
loss
of song

I can't recall

…The music
that I cannot make

for lack of everything

Only Snow Will Do

If that night could remember
it would call him back
to our Chinese restaurant
to fried rice and steaming tea
to our winter refuge of tile and cushions
'50s retro black and white
Chrome legs of lacquered tables
with its mural of *our* Great Wall

…winding, distant, wonder

If the snow hadn't muffled all
but our voices
we would not be—
so alone

Only I
felt his arm take it chance
around my shoulder
Guiding warmth
as good excuse as any
to touch

Two miles on foot
An arc in time
A lace of white to hide
what might…

From my window
"Goodbye"
not enough
for troubadour
singing, pleading, stumbling

(I worry about his long way home)

and hardly notice....

How gently Time joins Snow
as if they cannot bare
instead, conspire
Decide the crystals
Send the flakes to sift over him

This loss needs snow
to blur his face
to fade from view...

This—tender let-down from the sky
As only snow can do

Cover with beauty

Signed Her Name

Spring signed her name
with the breeze
Sipping the moon
from a goblet of budding trees

Gazed out across her path
Through the streets

By the houses of sleep?

Not in a hurry

Maybe no one will see her

slip into day
dressed in silence and silver

About the Author

Elizabeth Balise is a long-time resident of Scranton, Pennsylvania, who grew up in Springfield, Massachusetts. Most of her working life has been devoted to human services and to teaching English in public schools. Poetry entered as a teenager, but real love for it was fostered by her relationship with her Marywood College mentor, Barbara Hoffman.

A solitary writer, when not in front of a classroom, she filled journals and canvas bags with scraps of life, always thinking, "They must mean something?"

Her first publication was in the fall of 1989 issue of *The Endless Mountain Review.* Poems, short stories, and articles have appeared in ergo magazine of the old Prufrock's Cafe in Scranton, PA. One of her poems was selected for the anthology of the Mulberry Poets and Writers, *Palpable Clock,* University of Scranton Press. Online work has been published in *SWITCH* (2017), *Ariel Chart* (2020), *Thirteen Myna Birds* (2020), and also in *Mothers Aways Write* (October 2019).

She was a featured poet for the United States and Canada for *The Blue Nib* (September 2019).